WHAT IS TH
GUIDE FOR?
WHY ARE YOU
READING THIS?

This Guide is intended to be an introduction to Meshtastic for everyday folks. You don't have to be a computer person to understand how Meshtastic works, and the goal of this book is to make getting into Meshtastic as easy as using the cell phone that's already in your pocket! This Guide walks you through the concept of Meshtastic and then walks you through each step to set up your very own Meshtastic device. There's an example shopping list, a build guide, and pictures of each step as you get started with Meshtastic. **If you've ever been interested in Meshtastic or LoRa but thought it might be too hard, this guide was made for you.**

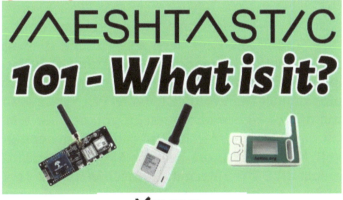

www.yavoz.tech

WHAT IS MESHTASTIC?

Hey there! Have you heard about Meshtastic? It's a really cool open-source project that uses LoRa (Long Range) radio technology to let people communicate over long distances without needing cell towers, Wi-Fi, internet, or any other infrastructure provided by any third parties at all. Imagine being out in the wilderness or during a power outage and still being able to send text messages to your friends; well, that's what Meshtastic does! Or imagine putting one in your car or your friend's cars and giving a few Meshtastic radios out to create a portable network on the go?

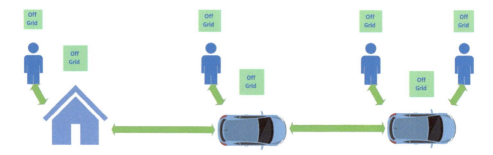

How far can a LoRa (Long Range) radio send a text message with Meshtastic? Some folks have been able to send messages as far as 157 miles; that's like sending a text from New York City to Philadelphia without needing anything other than two pocket-sized radios smaller than your cell phone. With the awesome LoRa Meshtastic line of sight radio range, if you can see a Meshtastic radio, you can talk to a Meshtastic radio. That would be great all by itself, but there's more because Meshtastic creates a Mesh network, just like the internet. A mesh network is a type of network where multiple devices, or nodes, are interconnected to communicate with one another. Unlike traditional networks that rely on a central hub (like a single router), each node in a mesh network can send and receive data, allowing for more flexible and reliable communication. Think of a mesh network like a group of friends at a party trying to share information. Instead of everyone having to go back to the host to get updates (which would be like relying on a central router), they can chat directly with each other. If one friend leaves the party (like a node going offline), the others can still pass messages along through different friends. This makes the communication much more resilient and efficient.

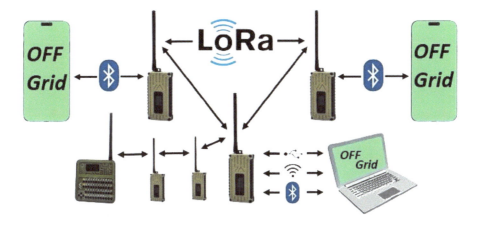

MESH NETWORK
KEY ADVANTAGES:

Here's an analogy to better explain the benefits of a mesh network. Imagine you're at a huge concert with your friends, and you all want to stay in touch. In a normal situation, you'd use your phones, right? But what if the cell towers are jammed because there are too many people? That's where Meshtastic comes in handy! Think of Meshtastic like a game of telephone, but way better. Each person with a Meshtastic device is like a player in the game. When you want to send a message, you don't have to yell across the whole crowd. Instead, you just whisper to the person next to you, and they pass it on to the next person, and so on, until it reaches your friend. The cool part is that everyone with a Meshtastic device becomes part of this chain. So even if your friend is way on the other side of the concert, your message can hop from person to person until it gets there. And the best part? You don't need cell service or Wi-Fi for this to work!

- **Reliability**: If one node fails, the others can still communicate, ensuring that the network remains operational.
- **Extended Range**: Messages can travel longer distances as they hop from one node to another, reducing dead zones

where signals might not reach.

- **Scalability**: You can easily add more nodes without disrupting the existing network, just like inviting more friends to join a conversation.
- **Self-Healing**: The network can automatically find new paths for data if connections are broken, similar to how friends would quickly adapt and find another way to share info.

But the LoRa Meshtastic range isn't the only cool feature. Imagine you have a gadget that can run for days or even weeks without needing to be charged; well, these little Meshtastic radios use so little power that you can. Even small batteries can keep these devices running for days or weeks, and if you attach a small USB solar charger to a Meshtastic radio, you can keep going forever without ever needing to plug it in. These devices can even take naps with smart features that, when they're not in use, can go into ultra-low-power sleep mode, waking up only occasionally to check if there are any messages. This low power consumption is super important because it means you can stay connected even when you're far away from civilization, during emergencies, or if you want your own private communication line like a superhero; even when the power goes out, you can still send messages to your friends.

REACHING ACROSS THE INTERNET WITH MQTT

Meshtastic also can use MQTT (Message Queuing Telemetry Transport) to connect different Meshtastic networks together over the Internet; it's a lightweight, publish-subscribe messaging protocol designed for efficient communication between devices, particularly in the Internet of Things (IoT) and machine-to-machine (M2M) applications. Meshtastic benefits from MQTT integration by expanding its capabilities for mesh networking because separate Meshtastic networks in different geographical locations can be connected over the Internet using an MQTT broker. Users can join their local mesh to a Meshtastic MQTT broker, making their devices visible on a global map. Private MQTT brokers can be used to cre
ate secure bridges between distant mesh networks. You can even set up encryption. Imagine you have Meshtastic networks in different cities or even countries. MQTT acts like a bridge, connecting these networks over the Internet with a secure tunnel with the help of a private MQTT broker. This means your devices can communicate across vast distances, way beyond the reach of their LoRa radios.

Meshtastic uses different encryption methods depending on the type of communication:

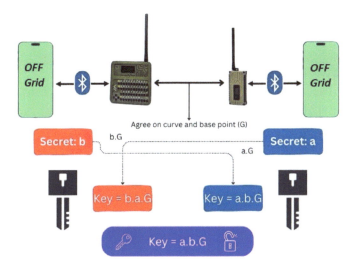

For Chat Channels:

- o   Meshtastic employs AES-CCM -256 bit encryption with a Pre-Shared Key (PSK).
- o   The encryption key is derived from the Channel name.
- o   All participants in a channel use the same PSK for encryption and decryption.

Imagine you and your friends have a secret treehouse club. To keep your conversations private, you all agree on a special code word - that's your channel name. Every time you want to send a message, you use this code word to scramble it up. It's like using an advanced version of those decoder rings you might find in a cereal box! Only the people who know the code word (your channel name) can unscramble the message. This way, even if someone overhears your conversation, all they'll hear is gibberish unless they know the secret code.

For Direct Messages (DMs):

- o   As of version 2.5.0, Meshtastic uses Public Key Cryptography (PKC).
- o   Each node has a unique public/private key pair.
- o   DMs are encrypted using the recipient's public key.

- ○ Messages are signed with the sender's private key before encryption.

Think of this like having a magical lockbox for each of your friends. You have the key to lock the box, but only your friend has the key to unlock it. When you want to send a secret message, you write it down, sign your name, put it in their special lockbox, and send it off. Even if someone intercepts the box, they can't open it - only your friend can. And when your friend opens it, they know it's from you because of your signature. It's a bit like sending a letter in a lockbox through the mail, where only the intended recipient has the key!

For Admin Messages:

- ○ Meshtastic uses a combination of PKC and Session IDs.
- ○ A Diffie-Hellman (DH) key exchange using Curve25519 generates a shared secret.
- ○ Subsequent communications use symmetric encryption (like AES-CTR or AES-CCM) with the shared secret.
- ○ Session IDs add an extra layer of security for each admin session.

Imagine you and your friend are master chefs creating a secret recipe together. Every time you cook, you start by mixing a unique blend of spices (that's your key exchange). You both contribute ingredients, but the final mix is something only you two know. This special spice blend becomes your secret ingredient for the entire cooking session. You use it to season all the dishes you make together (encrypt your messages). If someone else tries to taste your food, they can't figure out the secret spice blend. The best part? Next time you cook, you create a whole new spice mix. So even if someone guessed your old recipe, they're back to square one for your new cooking session. It's like having a new secret ingredient every time you step into the kitchen, making sure your culinary creations (your admin messages) stay top secret!

WHAT ARE MESSAGE HOPS?

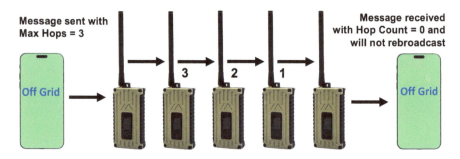

Message sent with Max Hops = 3

Message received with Hop Count = 0 and will not rebroadcast

Off Grid

Off Grid

Meshtastic uses hops to extend the range of communication beyond what a single device can achieve. Imagine you're playing a game of telephone, but instead of whispering, you're using Meshtastic devices to pass messages. Each person (or device) in this game is called a "node" in the Meshtastic network.

Message Relay:

When you send a message, your device doesn't just try to reach the final destination directly. Instead, it passes the message to nearby devices, which then pass it along to others, creating a chain of communication.

Hop Limit:

By default, Meshtastic sets a limit of 3 hops for each message. This means your message can be passed along up to 3 times before it stops being forwarded. It's like saying, "Pass this message on, but only 3 times!"

Extending Range:

Let's say your message can normally travel 1 mile. With 3 hops, it could potentially reach devices up to 3 miles away by "hopping" through other devices in between.

Customizable:

If you need your messages to travel further, you can increase the hop limit in the settings. But remember, more hops mean more devices handling your message, which can slow things down a bit.

Smart Routing:

Meshtastic devices are clever about how they pass messages. If a device hears that someone else has already passed along a message, it won't repeat it. This helps prevent unnecessary chatter on the network.

Acknowledgments:

When your message reaches its destination, you get a little "message received" notification. This happens even if your message had to hop through several other devices to get there.

By using hops, Meshtastic creates a network where devices work together to extend the range of communication. It's like having a team of your trusted friends passing your message along until it reaches its destination, even if that destination is far beyond what your device could reach on its own!

THE EXAMPLE SHOPPING LIST

The shopping list.

- In this example let's use a 3000mAh Lithium Rechargeable Battery with a Micro JST 1.25 Plug for an Arduino NodeMCU ESP32 Development Board.
https://amzn.to/4f1OlLy

- A MakerFocus Wireless Tracker ESP32 Development Board Integrated UC6580 SX1262 863 928MHz LoRa WiFi Bluetooth Support GPS GLONASS Multi System Joint Position with Display for Arduino Intelligent Scene
https://amzn.to/48t1ue0

- And a good 915MHz LoRa Antenna because the ones that come with the ESP32 are really low quality and performance. Getting a better antenna makes a world of difference.
https://amzn.to/4earADV

ASSEMBLING YOUR FIRST MESHTASTIC LORA RADIO

Once you've decided to build some radios and have purchased the components listed above it's time to start snapping things together. Don't worry, it's not hard at all. Start by laying out everything in front of you.

Once you've taken everything out of the box you'll be ready to start assembling everything together.

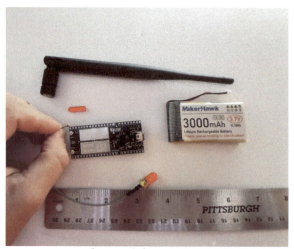

All the pieces snap together with JST 1.25 Plug connectors so it's easy.

The ESP32 development board says "LoRa" on it so you know what radio connection your plugin into.

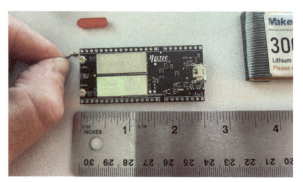

Go ahead and plug in the LoRa antenna to the ESP32 board. It snaps right on.

Next screw in the antenna to the connecting wire you just snapped onto the ESP32 development board.

CAUTION: Always connect an appropriate antenna to your Meshtastic ESP32 development board before applying power or turning on the device. Powering on the LoRa radio module without a properly connected antenna can cause permanent damage to the sensitive radio frequency (RF) components. The antenna serves as a crucial load for the transmitter output and helps dissipate the RF energy safely. Without this load, the energy can reflect back into the transmitter circuitry, potentially causing overheating and irreversible damage to the radio chip.

www.**yavoz**.tech

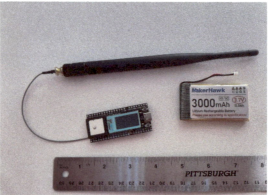

I chose to add an additional little GNSS antenna to assist with GPS, this isn't necessary but helps with GPS a little bit. If your kit came with an additional GNSS antenna then great and if not that's ok also.

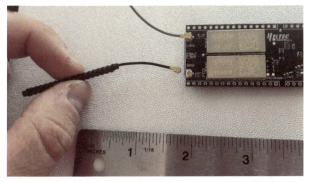

After you connect the required LoRa antenna and any additional optional GNSS antennas you may choose to add go ahead and connect the power from your battery to the ESP32 development board.

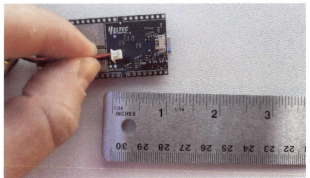

It snaps right in, easy as can be.

Once you have everything connected together your Meshtastic ESP32 development board will come to life.

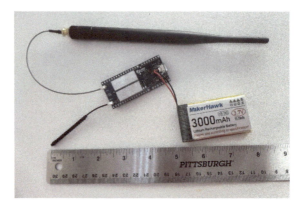

Once your Meshtastic ESP32 development board comes to life go ahead and plug it into your computer via the USB port.

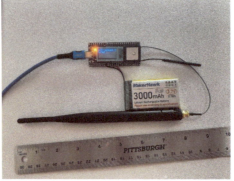

The next step is to go to the Web Flasher that Meshtastic themselves offer. There are other offline methods to flash the ESP32 development board with local software however the Meshtastic Web Flasher is the recommended method to install Meshtastic onto the ESP32 development board. The site to flash your ESP32 development board is **https://flasher.meshtastic.org/**

If you're not sure what device is the correct one you own, it will be written on the ESP32 development board itself.

In my case I'm using the Heltec wireless tracker V1.1 and I recommend under firmware selecting a stable version. I selected the latest stable version because I wanted all the latest features without any development bugs.

IMPORTANT: *The Meshtastic Web Flasher requires a Chromium-based browser for full functionality.*

Once you click the Flash button a window will pop up. Make sure the "Full Erase and Install" toggle switch is enabled. And click the green button that says Erase Flash and Install.

Once you do you will be asked what COM port your ESP32 development board is plugged into via USB. If you're not sure, unplug it and plug it back in, you'll notice one of the COM ports disappear and reappear, that is the COM port your ESP32 development board is plugged into via USB. On a windows computer you could also check your device manager to do the same check. Once you've selected your COM port you're ready to install Meshtastic to your ESP32 development board.

After the installation is complete **pat yourself on the back** and check your ESP32 development board to see that Meshtastic is installed.

Next download the Meshtastic app to your cell phone

Meshtastic
Meshtastic

Uninstall   Open

Once you have the App installed on your phone you can put your phone in airplane mode and only turn on Bluetooth to limit your phone to only communicate to the Meshtastic devices via bluetooth.

Next, connect your cell phone over bluetooth to your new Meshtastic device and start configuring your new Meshtastic device as much as you want.

Once you've finished having your initial excitement about your new awesome Meshtastic devices let's make some cases for them. You can create any case you want, in this case I 3D printed a case from https://www.printables.com/model/616628-heltec-wireless-tracker-case-for-meshtastic/files

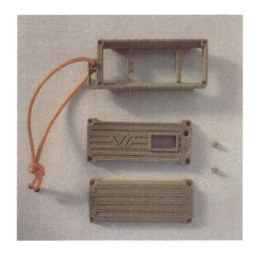

BASIC MESHTASTIC USER GUIDE

Welcome to the Meshtastic Android app! This handy tool helps you stay connected with your private group by showing everyone's location. Each member can see where others are, how far away they are, and even send and receive messages in your group chat.

When you first open the app, you'll see the Settings tab. Look for the little cloud icon with a slash through it in the upper right corner—that means your device isn't connected yet. Feel free to explore the tabs, but keep in mind that most features will be available once you connect to a Meshtastic radio. Happy exploring, and let's get connected!

First, make sure you have a device with Meshtastic installed. Now, let's find your Meshtastic device. For Bluetooth connections, simply tap the "+" button in the bottom right corner of the app. Using Wi-Fi or Ethernet? No problem! If your device is on the same network as your phone, it should pop up automatically and you also have the option to enter its IP address manually. There are lots of ways to connect to your new Meshtastic device. And if you prefer a direct connection, just plug your device into your phone with a USB cable. Your phone will spot it right away. Don't worry if it takes a try or two. You've got this!

Choose the device name, such as Meshtastic_769d in this example. You'll see a list of nearby devices, so be sure to select the correct one. To establish your first connection, you'll need to "pair" the devices, which enables them to communicate. You can configure your device to not require a PIN if you want to, by default it will ask you to enter a PIN displayed on the Meshtastic device's screen.

Important Note: If the device was flashed without a screen connected, it will automatically default to a pairing PIN of '123456'. If it was booted with a screen once, the config is set to a random pin. If you remove the screen afterwards, it stays like this. You can either set it to use the default pin manually, or factory reset it and it will revert to '123456' after the next boot.

This initiates the connection with the device, and the cloud icon in the status bar will change to display a check mark.

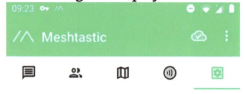

The cloud icon in the top right corner shows your connection status with a device and has three possible states:

- **Not Connected**:
  - A cloud with a slash through it means no device is currently connected to the app.

- **Connected**:
  - A cloud with a check mark indicates that your device is successfully connected to the app.

- **Sleeping**:
  - A cloud with an upward arrow signifies that the device is connected but is currently in sleep mode or out of range.

SET YOUR REGION

- To begin communicating with your mesh, you need to select a region. This setting determines the frequency range your device will use and should be adjusted based on your location. Below is a list of region codes and their meanings. Simply tap on the "Region" dropdown in the top-right corner and choose the option that matches your country. In my case I chose "US" because I live in the Great United States of America.

Region Code	Description	Frequency Range (MHz)	Duty Cycle (%)	Power Limit (dBm)
UNSET	Unset	N/A	N/A	N/A
US	United States	902.0 - 928.0	100	30
EU_433	European Union 433MHz	433.0 - 434.0	10	12
EU_868	European Union 868MHz	869.4 - 869.65	10	27
CN	China	470.0 - 510.0	100	19
JP	Japan	920.8 - 927.8	100	16
ANZ	Australia & New Zealand	915.0 - 928.0	100	30
KR	Korea	920.0 - 923.0	100	
TW	Taiwan	920.0 - 925.0	100	27
RU	Russia	868.7 - 869.2	100	20
IN	India	865.0 - 867.0	100	30
NZ_865	New Zealand 865MHz	864.0 - 868.0	100	36

TH	Thailand	920.0 - 925.0	100	16
UA_433	Ukraine 433MHz	433.0 - 434.7	10	10
UA_868	Ukraine 868MHz	868.0 - 868.6	1	14
MY_433	Malaysia 433MHz	433.0 - 435.0	100	20
MY_919	Malaysia 919MHz	919.0 - 924.0	100	27
SG_923	Singapore 923MHz	917.0 - 925.0	100	20
LORA_24	2.4 GHz band worldwide	2400.0 - 2483.5	100	10

GIVE YOUR MESHTASTIC DEVICE A UNIQUE NAME

Let's personalize your Meshtastic experience by setting up your device's name:

1. Find the "Your name" field and type in something unique, like "Mike Bird".
2. This is the name your group members will see, so pick something that stands out!
3. Your initials (like "MB") will be used in message history and on device screens, so make these unique too.
4. Want to customize your initials? Head over to Radio configuration > User settings to set a "short name".
5. You'll notice four characters after your initials - these are part of your device's unique ID and can't be changed.
6. If you don't set a name, your device will use these four

characters as its default short name.

Remember, a unique name helps everyone in your group know who's who. Make sure your Meshtastic identity is a cool name, because looking cool is 99% of the point.

LET'S SET UP YOUR MESHTASTIC CHANNELS

By default, your device comes with a preconfigured channel called #LongFast-I (Long range / Fast). This is great if you want to be visible to all nearby Meshtastic users on the default channel. However, if you're looking for more privacy, you can create a new channel and share its details with your group. This way, only those with the channel information can join and see messages. Don't worry, you only need to do this once when you start, or if you want to change or create a new mesh network group later. To get started, head to the Channel tab. You'll notice it's initially locked to prevent accidental changes. Just tap the lock symbol to unlock and edit. Then, you can select from various Channel options to find the one that best suits your needs. Remember, creating a private channel is a great way to keep your communications secure.

www. *Yavoz* .tech

After selecting the "Long Range / Fast" option, you can create a unique Channel Name for your group using the keyboard. For example, let's say you want to call your group "Owl Team." This name will help identify your private mesh network and allow only those with the channel details to join. Keep in mind that the Channel Name should be something memorable and meaningful to your group members. Once you've entered the name, your Meshtastic channel is all set up and ready for your team to start communicating securely and privately within your mesh network.

You'll receive a warning when changing the Channel, as doing so will disrupt communication with your group. This means that if you adjust your settings without sharing the new channel details with your team, they won't be able to connect with you. It's important to ensure that everyone in your group is informed of any changes to maintain seamless communication. The app will display a new QR code on the screen, which encodes the channel details along with a random 256-bit key for sharing with your new group. You can easily share this QR code with other Meshtastic users, or use the Share button to send the link via chat message, SMS, or email. Keep in mind that the link will be quite long, looking something like this: https://www.meshtastic.org/d/ #CgUYAyIBAQ. This makes it simple for your group members to connect and communicate securely.

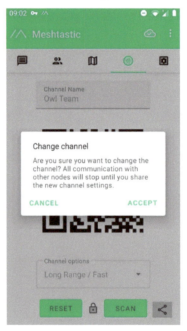

If another user shares a QR code, you can easily scan it directly with your camera by using the Scan button. This feature allows you to take a picture of their QR code to connect to their channel and join the conversation without any hassle. Just point your camera at the QR code, and you'll be all set. If someone shares a channel with you through a file or link using the Share button, you can easily join by simply clicking on the file or link. When prompted, make sure to select "Open with Meshtastic" to import the channel details into your app. This streamlined process allows you to quickly connect to shared channels and join the conversation with your group.

Important Note: *If a QR or URL opens a webpage instead of the APP or "Open with Meshtastic" is not an option:*

1. *Go to Android Settings > Apps > Default apps > Meshtastic > Opening links*
2. *Make sure you have in "links/web address": www.meshtastic.org*
3. *If you see the option "Open the supported links", make sure it is enabled.*

Next, a message will appear asking, "Do you want to switch to the 'Owl Team' channel?" If you accept this prompt, the app will transition to the new channel. Keep in mind that doing so will result in the loss of any current channel settings you have in place.

HOW TO SEND A MESSAGE

Sending messages in the Meshtastic app is similar to most messaging apps you're familiar with. Your primary channel, like LongFast, acts as a group chat and is always visible. For direct messaging or private group chats, you can use other contacts. To access additional options like delete, simply long-press on contacts or messages. You can also send Direct Messages by tapping on a node from the Nodes tab. Given the nature of LoRa (and radio communication in general), there's some uncertainty about message delivery. That's why the app includes built-in confirmation features.

You'll notice small icons next to your sent messages that indicate their status:

- Cloud with an up arrow: Your message is queued in the app, waiting to be sent to the device.
- Cloud only: The device has received the message from the

app and transmitted it via LoRa.

- Cloud with a check mark: At least one node has acknowledged receiving the message.
- Person with a check mark: The intended recipient of your direct message has acknowledged it.
- Cloud crossed out: The sender didn't receive any confirmation within the set timeout period.

It's important to note that by default, there's no long-term store-and-forward system for messages. This means that if a message isn't received during transmission, it's lost. Keep this in mind when communicating over longer distances or in challenging conditions.

HOW TO VIEW OTHERS IN YOUR NETWORK

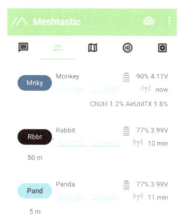

The network list in your Meshtastic app provides a comprehensive view of all users (devices) connected to the same Channel. Each entry displays valuable information such as the user's last active time, location, distance (when available), and their most recent power status. For instance, in the example given, you can see that Monkey is the local user, Rabbit was last active 10 minutes ago and is 50m away, while Panda was last heard from 11 minutes ago at a distance of 5m. To interact with the network list, you have several options. Tapping on a node reveals more detailed information about that user, and you can toggle the Show Details option in the filter menu for an expanded view. For quick actions, tap on a node's colored chip to start Direct Messaging, request a position update, initiate a traceroute, or add the node to your Ignore Incoming Array. If you need location information, tapping on a node's coordinates will open your preferred maps application, while a long press copies the coordinates to your clipboard. Additionally, if you have an Admin Channel enabled on your devices, tapping the node's colored chip will provide an option to remotely configure that node. This feature-rich interface allows you to easily manage and interact with your Meshtastic network.

USING THE MAP

The Map tab displays a local map featuring an icon for each active mesh node with a known position. Above each icon, you'll see the corresponding user's name. To customize your view, simply click on the layers icon in the top-right corner, where you can choose from different map types to suit your preferences. This makes it easy to visualize your network and keep track of all active users in your area.

Some map types let you download maps for offline use, which can be particularly useful in areas with limited connectivity. If offline maps are available for your selected map type, you'll notice a download icon in the bottom-right corner of the map. To download a region for offline access, tap the icon and choose the "Download Region" option. You'll then be prompted to select the specific area you want to download, ensuring you have access to the map data even when an internet connection is unavailable.

GOING FURTHER
WITH MESHTASTIC

Although beyond the scope of this guide you can do a lot more with these devices like combine it with ATAC. I recommend you check out this linked video to learn a lot more about how these devices can be used. https://www.youtube.com/watch?v=mb2OBIw-1Oc

SETTING MESHTASTIC ROLES

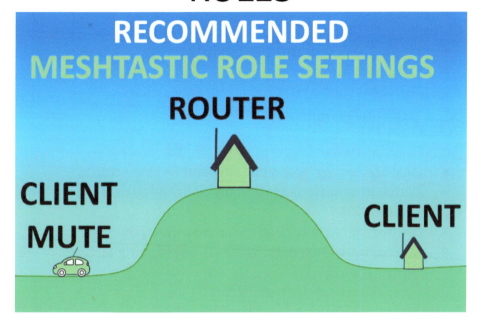

CLIENT ROLES

Meshtastic offers several device roles that group together configuration settings for different use cases. The main roles include:

CLIENT

- This is the default role for most users
- Enables communication via Bluetooth and app
- Re-routes traffic picked up from other nodes
- Recommended for general use

CLIENT_MUTE

- Recommended for portable nodes like in vehicles
- Picks up nearby nodes but does not re-route traffic
- Helps prevent issues caused by poor re-routing

CLIENT_HIDDEN

- Only broadcasts as needed for stealth or power savings
- Useful for hidden deployments or reducing airtime/power consumption

Infrastructure Roles

ROUTER

- Used to extend network coverage
- Visible in node lists
- Should be placed at vantage points with clear line of sight
- Misuse can cause routing issues

REPEATER

- Extends coverage but not visible in node lists
- Also requires optimal placement at vantage points

Specialized Roles

TRACKER

- Prioritizes broadcasting GPS position packets
- Useful for tracking assets or individuals

SENSOR

- Prioritizes broadcasting telemetry data
- Ideal for environmental monitoring deployments

TAK
- Optimized for ATAK system communication
- Reduces routine broadcasts

It's generally recommended to use the CLIENT role unless you have a specific reason to use another role. Proper role selection helps optimize network performance and stability.

ABOUT THE AUTHOR

Kie Yavorsky who goes by the name "Yavo" is the creator of www.yavoz.tech and this guide. He is a cyber security specialist with over 14 years of IT experience who served as a Sergeant in the United States Marine Corps from 2009 to 2017, filling cyber security roles including Cyber Chief, Firewall Admin, Network Engineer, Server Admin, Satcom Admin, Radio Admin, Crypto Electronic Key Management System (EKMS) Manager, SharePoint Webmaster, IT Project Manager and Cyber Security Expert. He has been recognized for leading the communication plan of 266th Pope, Pope Francis to the National Capital Region and the 2011 Presidential State of the Union Address, while stationed at Chemical Biological Incident Response force (CBIRF) in Washington DC. Yavo was also recognized during Operation Key Resolve, Cobra Gold, and other operations in the Asia-Pacific region supporting tens of thousands of users while serving in Okinawa Japan. Yavo then became the Cyber Chief of the infantry battalion 3rd Battalion, 4th Marines. The unit holds the nicknames "Thundering Third" and "Darkside". After the Marine Corps Yavo has received multiple innovation and performance awards in his civilian career serving in roles to include Network Operations Lead in Iwakuni Japan, Lead Network Engineer for Defense Information Systems Agency (DISA), Information System Security Officer (ISSO) for the Nuclear Intercontinental Ballistic Missile (ICBM) Minute Man III program In Ogden Utah, Risk Management Framework (RMF) Security Control Assessor (SCA) for AFRICOM, and Information System Security Officer (ISSO) for EUCOM in Stuttgart Germany, and an Information System Security Officer (ISSO) for the Air Force Enterprise IT as a Service (EITaaS) Program. His education includes a Master's Degree in Cybersecurity and Information Assurance from Western Governors University and a Bachelor's Degree in Cyber Security with two concentrations, the first concentration in Information Warfare, and the second concentration in Cyber Connections Management from Norwich University. His industry certifications include the Certified Information Systems Security Professional (CISSP), Certified Ethical Hacker (CEH), CompTIA Cybersecurity Analyst (CySA+), CompTIA Security+, Cisco Certified Network Professional

Enterprise (CCNP - Enterprise), Cisco Certified Specialist - Enterprise Core, Cisco Certified Specialist - Enterprise Advanced Infrastructure Implementation, Cisco Certified Network Associate (CCNA) and 44 other IT cyber security training certifications. Yavo is continuously innovating and very passionate about cyber security, leading others, and working as a mentor to aspiring IT professionals. He spends his time volunteering with the Young Marine Youth Program, participating in the Experimental Aircraft Association (EAA) as he builds aircraft in his garage, 3D printing, providing security for his local Church, recreational shooting, Jujitsu, muay thai, camping, and most importantly spending time with his family, they often watching anime together after a long day of fun.

www.*Yavoz*.tech